I'm so happy you've decided to explore the Canna way of eating with me. Legally we can't make any medical claims with cannabis, cooking with cannabis or cannabis infused products. Everyone has their own methods. Here are a few ideas to try.

For a very long time I've wanted to share ideas. I felt like a prisoner trapped in mediocrity, I felt like my ideas weren't good enough. Instead of blaming others I'm taking back my power. The worst mistake I've ever made was not thinking big enough.

Often the college kid (Malik) would text me asking for my spaghetti recipe or my chili recipe. Although those two aren't included in this book, I have some pretty amazing ones in here. I can't say which are my favorite but please feel free to share with me which one becomes yours.

-Thank you for your purchase

Victoria LP

Victoria LP Present......Cooking with a twist

ACC OF Illinois Edition

Copyright © 2020 by Victoria Williams

Victoria LP *Presents*

Cooking with a Twist

COOKBOOK FOR CANNABIS-INFUSED
MEALS AND DESSERTS

INCLUDING "INFUSED" RECIPES FOR:

BUTTER aka CANNABUTTER · BAKED APPLE FRENCH TOAST · HOT WINGS
BAKED MAC & CHEESE W/ BACON · SWEET POTATO PIE
HARD CANDY · POUND CAKE

ACC
ACC Edition
WWW.ACCOFILLINOIS.COM

Victoria LP *Presents*

Cooking with a Twist

ACC
ACC Edition

To my three broke best friends
"Christian, Calvin, and Bryce"

Make speak with integrity, only say what you mean. Don't take anything personally, don't assumptions and always, always do your very best. My true strength came from being your mother.

To My Mom
"Angela"

We have our own special story. It has never been a time in my life that I needed you that you were not there. From childbirth to heart breaks you have taught me to never look at a loss as a loss but a lesson. Trust me I've learned from each. Thank you, Mom.

To My Sister and Brother
"Lakeisha and John"

It was not very easy breaking into the ground floor of this industry. Thank you for no judgement and always being a call away.

To My Younger Brother
"Malik"

You are the youngest of the group. I often looked at you like you were my first Son. I want to thank you for allowing me to use your special recipe to infused into a masterpiece. I placed my bet on you from day one and told our mom to put all our money on you. The first to be inducted into the national honor society, the first to go to a D1 school, I remember the tears I cried when you walked that high school stage and here we are in your Junior year of college beating the odds. I'm just proud to be your sister.

To My Friends;

Mesha, Necole M., Whitney, Aubrey C., Aubrey P., Joi, Donald, Ray, Tinisha, Erika, Dominique, Kenneth, Amy, Marcus, Jasmine, Cliff (cousin), Chiquita, WAK Andre, Walter, Esther, Ethel, Angela (O.E.S),

You guys has seen me through some of the lowest points in my life and consistently checked on me for years. I value our friendship so much. Thank you for all for being great friends.

Special appreciation to

Cooking with a twist - 6

"Chavonne"

Thank you for not standing behind me but beside me. you tell me consistently how I lit a fire under you when you actually kept me from blowing mine out.

My firm is ACC of Illinois. ACC is dedicated to training dispensary owners and associates regarding the best practices according to the law. ACC aids and supports owners with growth and the development of their business. To date, ACC has held several training seminars to assist veterans, social equity and other individuals to obtain their Dispensary Agent Training certification.

ACC Of Illinois is approved to train in multiple City's within the State of Illinois. With Offices located in Chicago, Oak Forest, and Aurora Illinois. ACC also provides online training and one in one support as needed.

I, Victoria LP co-authored the ACC of Illinois training manual which details the 610-page HB1438 law into comprehensive language, which can be easily understood by all levels of management and employees. One of my goals is to assist the disenfranchised and marginalize people of ethnic communities to succeed in an industry which criminalized them prior to the passing of the law.

Also, I am a serial entrepreneur with several businesses and I'm a certified CPR/First-Aid instructor that provides lifesaving training to clients.

Table of Contents

Cannabis-infused ancillary products are the most sought-after marijuana Products in legalized marijuana marketplaces. Ancillary products are now representing over 62% of the overall marijuana market. Most infused products companies have created a recognizable brand for legal age purchasers and medical cannabis patients through precision dosing, tasteless and odorless confectionary or extremely potent products.

Extraction and infusion create additional revenue opportunities through numerous additional product lines, including concentrates, wax, vapor cartridges, Topical and other concepts still in development.

Operations:

Converting raw materials into infused products: Operational needs include Cultivation of raw materials, a supply of pre-manufactured substrates, extraction through a closed loop n-butane system, infusion through a proprietary process that requires minimal working space, storage of a pre-infused substrate and infused goods, and order fulfillment through an in-house proprietary system that works with the state tracking system.

1. 1-lb of unsalted butter (4 sticks)
2. 2g of THC Shatter (Top Grade)
3. 1- Pyrex bowl with top
4. 1- Whisk
5. 1- pair of gloves

Let's cook with a twist:

- ✓ In a non-stick pot add butter. Allow butter to melt completely but not boil. Once butter has melted add shatter. Be sure to wear gloves (Do not touch shatter with bare hands) using a whisk stir shatter into butter (No more than 4 minutes).
- ✓ Pour cooked canna butter into Pyrex bowl. Cover. Allow to cool. Then refrigerate.
- ✓ Discharge gloves.

Note:

- ➢ 1g of shatter is 1,000mg
- ➢ 2g of shatter is 2,000mg
- ➢ 2g of shatter in one pound of butter (4 sticks)
- ➢ Be Mindful each stick of butter is 500mg

➢ 8 tablespoons/ 62.5mg per teaspoon.

Infused Baked Apple French Toast

1. 1-loaf French bread
2. 1- can nonstick cooking spray
3. 8-large eggs, slightly beaten
4. 3- ½ cups 2%milk
5. 1- Cup of sugar divided
6. 1- tablespoon vanilla extract
7. 6- medium apples, peeled and thinly sliced
8. 3- teaspoons ground cinnamon
9. 1- teaspoon ground nutmeg
10. 1- tablespoon Canna butter

Let's cook with a twist:

✓ Slice bread into 1 ½ inch slices. Coat a 9 x 13-inch pan with nonstick cooking spray and tightly pack bread into pan.
✓ In a large bowl, stir eggs, milk, ½ cup of sugar and vanilla. Pour half the egg mixture over the bread slices.
✓ Evenly distribute apple slices over bread. Top with remaining egg mixture.
✓ In a small bowl combine remaining ½ cup sugar, the cinnamon and nutmeg. Sprinkle over apples.

Dot with Canna-butter. Cover and refrigerate overnight.

✓ Next day, uncover pan and bake in a preheated 350-degree oven for 1 hour. Remove from oven and let stand got 10-15 minutes. Cut and serve.

1. 12-ounce box of elbow macaroni
2. 2 Eggs
3. 3 tablespoons of unsalted Canna butter
4. 1 ½ cups Milk
5. 8 oz of shredded cheddar cheese (2 cups)
6. 2 strips of Bacon
7. 1 teaspoon salt
8. 1 teaspoon of pepper
9. 1 teaspoon of sugar

Let's cook with a twist:

✓ Pre heat oven to 375. Cook the macaroni in a large pot of boiling water until tender not mushy maybe 9 minutes. Drain very well, place in a mixing bowl. In a separate skillet fry two pieces of bacon. Cook well on both side until crispy. Remove from skillet allow grease to drain completely.

✓ Mix macaroni with remaining ingredients reserving ¼ cup of milk and cheese. Transfer to a 11-inch baking dish. Pour the reserve milk on top then add the reserved cheese.

Take cooking shears cut cooked bacon into pieces sprinkle on top.

✓ Bake 25 minutes or until top is golden brown and bubbling. Serve Hot.

Burning Hot Wing Malik Robinson Original
Recipe with an ACC twist

1. 1 bottle Red franks hot sauce
2. 1 tablespoon salt
3. 1 tablespoon pepper
4. 1 tablespoon cayenne
5. 1 tablespoon garlic powder
6. 1 tablespoon paprika
7. All purpose flour
8. Vegetable oil
9. Canna-butter

Sauce ingredients:

- 1/2 cup Red franks
- 2 Tbs Canna-butter
- 2 Tbs Brown sugar
- 1 Tbs Sugar
- 1/3 cup Ketchup
- 1 Tbs Salt
- 4 Tbs Cayenne
- 2 Tbs Black Pepper
- 2 Tbs Smoke paprika

Let's cook with a twist:

Cooking with a twist - 18

✓ Begin by taking 2lbs of chicken and washing them clean, using vinegar, lemon juice and water should help sanitize your chicken.

✓ Pat your chicken dry with a paper towel (this is important btw) to remove access moisture and place them in a clean bowl.

✓ Take the bottle of red franks hot sauce and begin to vigorously drip just enough hot sauce for you to cover, rub chicken together till every piece has a dark orange/red color.

✓ Begin seasoning your chicken with all of the seasoning ingredients, rub together to marinate well and place in fridge as you heat up fresh vegetable oil to 375 degrees.

✓ Take a zip bloc bag and fill it up half way with the flour and add all the seasonings again EXCEPT the salt. Once the grease is hot enough for cooking (375 degrees) take your chicken and shake him up in the zip bloc bag until evenly coated. Then drop him in the fryer and cook till 165 degrees 15-20mins.

✓ Once all the chicken has cooked take a small sauce pot and begin to add Canna-butter from the sauce ingredient(s) list and let it melt then proceed by adding the hot sauce and ketchup from the list.

✓ Once everything is at a small boil and begin to thicken it's time to add all of the remaining seasoning from the sauce ingredient(s) list then return to a boil one more time before turning off.

✓ Taste test at this point, you should have a spicy/ tangy and sweet bust of flavor in your mouth once you try your sauce. If anything is too spicy or too sweet just adjust the amount of cayenne or sugar used.

Infused Suckers

1. 2/3 Cups of light corn syrup
2. 1 Cup water
3. 2 Cups of sugar
4. Food Coloring
5. Flavoring
6. Molds
7. Sticks
8. Candy Thermometer

Let's cook with a twist:

✓ Add water, sugar, and corn syrup and Stir.

✓ Wait for sugar to dissolve Add candy thermometer.

✓ After your candy has reached 300 degrees remove from heat add food coloring stir rapidly Add flavoring stir and pour.

✓ Allow to fully cool before serving.

If making candy spray a lite pam into molds very lite, pour, cool, served.

1. 1 cup white sugar
2. 1 cup canna butter
3. 1 egg
4. 2 2/3 cups all purpose flour
5. ¼ teaspoon salt
6. 2 teaspoons vanilla extract

Let's cook with a twist:

✓ In mixing bowl, cream together the butter and white sugar until light and fluffy. Beat in egg, and then stir in vanilla.

✓ In separate bowl combine flour and salt; stir into sugar mixture. Cover dough, place in refrigerator for 1 hour

✓ Preheat oven 400 degrees F. Press dough out onto ungreased, chilled cookie sheet. Bake for 8 to 10 minutes or until lightly golden brown at the edges.

Infused Peanut Butter Cookies

1. 1 cup crunchy peanut butter
2. 1 cup canna butter
3. 1 cup granulated white sugar
4. 1 cup brown sugar
5. 2 eggs
6. 2 ½ cup flour
7. ½ teaspoon salt
8. 1 teaspoon of baking powder
9. 1 ½ teaspoon baking soda

Let's cook with a twist

✓ Pre heat oven 375 In a mixing bowl cream butter, peanut butter, and sugars; beat in eggs.

✓ In a separate bowl, sift flour, baking powder, baking soda, and salt; stir into butter mixture. Put dough in refrigerator for 1 hour.

✓ Roll dough into 1" balls and put on baking sheets. Flatten each ball with a fork, making crisscross pattern. Bake in preheated 375 degrees F oven for about 10 minutes or until cookies begin to brown.

Infused Pound Cake

1. 2 cups (4 sticks) unsalted Canna-butter, softened
2. 3 cups of cake flour
3. 3 ½ cups of sugar
4. 8 large eggs
5. 1 cup of heavy cream or milk
6. 2 tablespoons vanilla extract

Let's cook with a twist

✓ Preheat oven to 350. Add a little Canna-butter and flour to 9 x 4 ½ loaf pan

✓ Beat Canna-butter in a bowel with a mixer until soft. Gradually add sugar, continue beating until very light and fluffy. Add eggs one at a time while continuously beating. When they thoroughly blended, add the flour one cup at a time while beating at a low speed until blended. Stir in cream and vanilla.

✓ Pour the batter into the loaf pan and bake 1 ½ hours until golden brown and a cake tester/ toothpick comes out clean. Allow to cool for about 10 minutes, remove from the cake from the pan, cool it completely before serving.

1. 1 10 inch pie shell
2. 2 ½ cups of mashed cooked sweet potatoes
3. 8 tablespoons (1 stick) unsalted Canna-butter, softened
4. 1 ¾ cups sugar
5. 1 teaspoon ground nutmeg
6. 1 teaspoon vanilla extract
7. 2 large eggs
8. 1 7-ounce can evaporated milk

Let's Cook with a twist:

✓ Make the pie shell and cool it. Reduce oven to 300 degrees

✓ Beat the sweet potatoes and Canna-butter with an electric mixer until smooth. Add sugar, nutmeg, and vanilla. Add in eggs one at a time beating well after each. Add milk beating continuously.

✓ Add pie filling to a cool pie crust and smooth the top with spoon. Bake for about 35-40.

We procured companies that are either currently in the cannabis business or will be potentially entering the cannabis space and partnering with them to establish scholarships for people who live in disproportionately impacted areas. Through the program we directly affect impacted areas by providing spending power to those areas created by the job opportunities a recipient receives upon the completion of the Dispensary Agent Training.

Each student potentially is $2,400 in spending power per month.Each company provided 10 scholarships accounting for $24,000 per month in spending power in an economically depressed area and $288,000 in a year's span.

4 companies provided a total of 40 scholarships accounting for minimum 1.1 million of spending power in an economically depressed area.

There are many positives

• Management Opportunities

• Expungement

Cooking with a twist - 28

- Sponsored Dispensary Agent Training
- Application assistance
- Job placement opportunities
- A chance to obtain a job above the living wage of
- Companies that can help you facilitate your next career move

One of the reasons the program was formed was due to the lack of information that was being distributed in the disproportionately impacted areas where many of the dispensaries will open. We basically have a situation where an entire industry had been dropped in our state with little to no preparation or information to disproportionately impacted residents. There was no plan or resource made available to those who could potentially own or work in the cannabis industry. There was essentially no information in regard to banking or alternatives such as financing and credit.

We decided to take on the challenge of diversifying the Illinois cannabis industry through our grassroots efforts and community events that we have orchestrated.

About ACC:

Our story so far 55 Social Equity Applicants has been trained for free. 25 Veterans also have been trained and certified for free by ACC OF ILLINOIS

Over the Thanksgiving 2019 holiday weekend 55 individuals received scholarships for Dispensary Agent Training. In addition to receiving scholarships, they were able to apply for Jobs with 5 different sponsoring companies on site.

Let's do some math. As we all know most Dispensary's pay an hourly rate plus tips.

Hypothetically, if a dispensary, or cultivation center, or processing plant pay an employee $17 per hour.

Cooking with a twist - 30

$17/hour in a 40-hour work week is $680 per week. Multiplied by 4 is $2,720/month. Multiplied by 12 is $32,640/yr. Multiplied by 10 is $326,400 pumped back into the community. Let's take $32,640/year multiplied by 55 individuals. $1,795,200 Economic power is being pumped back into your very own neighborhood

This Is Social Equity. Congratulations to all who took advantage of this opportunity to be trained by ACC of Illinois #acctrained

We are pleased to announce ACC OF Illinois DISPENSARY AGENT TRAINING TOUR

Find training from an Illinois Approved Responsible Vendor in a City near You!

- January 8,2020-CTS Oak Forest Illinois
- January 11,2020- Chicago
- January 13, 2020- Prairie State College
- January 14,2020- DENVER CO Dispensary Tour
- January 18,2020- Evanston, Illinois
- January 25,2020- Aurora, Illinois
- January 27,2020- Prairie State College
- January 29,2020- CTS 150th Cicero

- February 8,2020 - Champagne Illinois
- February 15,2020- Springfield, Illinois
- February 22,2020 Aurora Illinois
- March 7, 2020- Springfield Illinois
- Link to training manuals

ACC Illinois Dispensary Training Manual
https://www.amazon.com/dp/1088552692/ref=cm_
sw_r_cp_api_i_uejdEb334NR7Q

www.accofillinois.com

Victoria is originally from the Chicagoland area born and raised. She has worked extensively in the cannabis industry to create businesses and opportunities for others in the cannabis industry. In the last 6 years she and her partners within ACC of Illinois have developed multiple

educational platforms where people can receive cannabis training to participate in the cannabis industry. ACC of Illinois is the first company awarded trusted vendor licensing for cannabis education in Illinois.

People can receive training in person, online, or through our micro cannabis education program. Victoria has developed digital content for ACC of Illinois as well as multiple clients. Victoria has also created an educational platform for people who were/are not in the cannabis industry to become involved in the cannabis industry whether it is working in the cannabis field or the ownership aspect of the cannabis industry.

While in the cannabis industry Victoria has written 3 cannabis business related books that are available through Walmart, Amazon, as well as ACC of Illinois website.

Victoria while trying to figure out how to get more social equity applicants involved in the Illinois cannabis industry developed a cannabis tour in Denver, Colorado. By creating this program, it allowed potential applicants:

• To see the size and scope of a dispensary and processing facility

• Speak to actual owners of cannabis companies

• Actual cost analysis of business

• Networking with owners and potential owners in the cannabis industry

Through creating classes to educate and workshops to inform people who reside in an economically disproportionate area, she and ACC of Illinois have created many owners and potential employees in the

Illinois cannabis industry and have inspired many others to want to participate in the cannabis industry.

Education:

Our company developed 6 classes that we have been teaching for 5 years. The 6 classes are:

- Infusion 101
- Cooking Candy with Cannabis
- Trimming 101
- Dispensary Agent Training
- Cultivation at Home (Medical)
- Introduction to Grow

Hands-on training: We provide hands on training to create these infused items listed below.

- Canna-Butter
- Infused Honey
- Infused Oil
- Infused Lollipops
- Infused Gummies

Made in the USA
Monee, IL
29 July 2021